WILDLIFE IN DANGER

by

Ivah Green

Illustrated with photographs

Would you like to see the bald eagle in flight, his great wings stretched out against the sky? Or the magnificent bighorn sheep perched high on a rocky mountain ledge? Would you like to hear the call of the trumpeter swan or the strange buglelike blasts that give the whooping crane his name? These are birds and animals you will probably never see, as they are among 29 species that are either extinct or threatened with extinction. Everyone interested in wildlife and in preserving rare birds and animals will get a picture here of what has been done for conservation and what still must be done to save those wilderness inhabitants that still remain.

* * * *

Dewey Decimal Classification: 333.7

About the Author:

IVAH GREEN is actively concerned about our vanishing wildlife. Miss Green teaches courses in education and children's literature at Doane College in Crete, Nebraska, and also works with many conservation organizations. For the past ten years she has included wildlife conservation in her annual conservation workshop for teachers at Doane College.

WILDLIFE
IN
DANGER

by Ivah Green

with Introduction by

Robert Porter Allen

1964 FIRST CADMUS EDITION
THIS SPECIAL EDITION IS PUBLISHED BY ARRANGEMENT WITH
THE PUBLISHERS OF THE REGULAR EDITION
COWARD-McCANN, INC.
BY
E. M. HALE AND COMPANY
EAU CLAIRE, WISCONSIN

To

Laurel, Candace, Jack, Jimmy, and Diana

© 1960 by Ivah Green

Library of Congress Catalog Card Number: 60-6108

This edition lithographed in U. S. A. by Wetzel Bros., Inc., Milwaukee 2, Wisconsin

Contents

INTRODUCTION

It is my firm belief that if books like the present one might have been read by children two or three generations ago, most of the endangered birds and mammals described here would today be abundant and free from current threats. It is even possible that birds now extinct would still be alive. But looking to the future, we can be glad that the children of today will be better informed on these matters than were their parents and grandparents. Out of this happy circumstance will come a better world in which to live, for in spite of the many gadgets and insulations of modern life, man is still a child of nature, and cannot live too far removed from it if he is to be content.

The pioneer days, when we fought to overcome nature, are long gone. We now have the leisure, and let us hope the good sense, to understand more clearly the natural world in which we live, and to help preserve its many wonders for future generations.

Robert Porter Allen

In my teens, the mere glimpse of a bird would change my listlessness to fierce intensity. I lived for birds. There are youngsters today whose eyes light up the same way at the sight of a bird. And so it will always be.

ROGER TORY PETERSON

Great White Heron

~~~~~~

OF OUR NUMEROUS species of heron, the great white heron is the largest in size, and the rarest. Perhaps he is also the most beautiful, in his immaculately white plumage, which contrasts sharply with his yellow-green bill and legs. He is often confused with the American egret, but the American egret is a smaller bird, with black legs.

Great white herons live close to salt water. They build flat nests of sticks, about three feet in diameter in black mangrove trees close to the shore or in bushes a few feet

Max Hunn
National Audubon Society

above the high-water mark. Parent birds take turns sitting on the nest while eggs are being incubated.

The great white heron has a loud raucous alarm note which he sounds frequently. He walks slowly and with dignity as he feeds in the shallow salt water. He eats mainly fish. He does not pursue his prey but stands motionless until it comes near him. Then he reaches down and seizes it in his bill and swallows it alive if it is small. If it is large he shakes it violently or beats it on the water to kill it.

Great white herons have been killed off in great numbers. In flight they made a tempting target for hunters. Their nests were plundered by sponge fishermen who wanted to eat the eggs. This loss of eggs caused a reduction in the number of young herons hatched each year. Their nesting habitat is the mangrove growth, and often birds, nests, eggs, and young were destroyed in the violent hurricanes that commonly swept over the area.

It is estimated that as many as two thousand or more great whites are in existence today, almost entirely in Florida Bay and the Florida Keys. They are protected in three areas: Everglades National Park, the Great White Heron National Wildlife Refuge, and the Key West National Wildlife Refuge.

After being "shot" by a camera, an animal continues to live its natural, happy life, to raise its young, and to give enjoyment to other people who see it. If you must shoot, do it with a camera.

DEVEREUX BUTCHER

Wood Duck

~~~~~~

THE MALE wood duck is one of the most beautiful of all waterfowl. Iridescent feathers of green and purple on his crest, back, and wings are accented by lines of white. His underparts are red, yellow, and white. His feet and bill are red. The female is brown above and yellowish white below.

The range of the wood duck was originally all of temperate North America, but he lives and migrates mainly within the United States. More than any other duck he is a woodland bird, frequenting ponds and streams bordered by woods. Wood ducks differ from other ducks in that they nest in tree cavities, sometimes holes made by woodpeckers. They lay from eight to 15 eggs which hatch in about a month, and when the young ones are one or two days old, the mother takes them to the water.

At one time in our country the wood duck was plentiful. A man who saw great numbers of them in Ohio in 1896 reported that it was possible to walk for a hundred miles without leaving the forest, and that the ponds and creeks in and around those forests were swarming with waterfowl, most of them wood ducks.

For many years wood ducks were hunted by men for their flesh, which is delicious; for their beauty when stuffed and put on display; and for their feathers to make flies for salmon and trout fishing. Hunters got a good price from fishermen for wood duck feathers, sometimes as much as four dollars for the whole skin of a male wood duck.

Wood ducks are friendly birds and they like to live close to people. They have always been easy marks for hunters' guns. These birds were also trusting. They could be decoyed easily by hunters who awaited them in blinds and shot them by hundreds. The ducks were sold in open markets for as little as ten cents a duck.

In some states there were no laws that forbade wood duck hunting. Men could shoot them at any time. Hunters lay in wait for the wood ducks to pass north on their spring

Devereux Butcher

migration flights to rear families of young. So many female ducks were killed that the wood duck population began to decrease at an alarming rate.

These friendly creatures faced other dangers. Like all waterfowl, their great need was for water. Water wasn't always easy to find, for many places that had once held water had been drained so that men could do more farming and stock raising. Thousands of shallow lakes and swamps were drained into ditches along roadsides. This meant that millions of acres of natural water reservoirs were no longer available for waterfowl.

In addition to the loss of water sources, the wood ducks were affected by drought. So little rain fell during one ten-year period that many streams and lakes dried up. Thousands of ducklings died. Those that lived and yet were unable to fly were killed by predators. Each fall fewer and fewer wood ducks made their migratory journey south; many of those who did were killed by hunters. Each spring fewer and fewer wood ducks returned north to find nesting sites.

Those who did return found a lack of nesting places. The trees, like the water, were fast disappearing. Thousands of trees were cut down in huge logging operations. Thousands were burned up in raging fires. Because of the lack of suitable nesting places, fewer and fewer wood ducks were hatched each year. These beautiful birds faced extinction.

People who were concerned about the possible fate of this harmless species of wildlife worked to make conditions more favorable for its existence. State and Federal laws were passed forbidding the shooting of wood ducks at any time. In some places drained areas were allowed to become swamp again where wood ducks could swim and feed. Refuges were established in which wood ducks were protected. Thousands of man-made nesting boxes were put up to encourage the wood ducks to lay their eggs in them. Wood ducks are now making a comeback. In most states there is an open season for them (limit of one per day per hunter). But they are still in need of help and protection.

Kit Fox

~~~~~~

SMALLEST of all the foxes, the "kit" seems more like a small cat. The small body is offset by large, prominent ears, which are of great help to this fox in locating his prey. He is slenderly built, with gray or buff-gray fur, sometimes with a touch of yellow. He weighs about four pounds.

His ability to run swiftly is another help to this little fox. Fastest of all the foxes, he can overtake and seize fast-moving animals such as kangaroo rats, jack rabbits, and ground squirrels. His speed is a help, too, in escaping from those who would prey on him — dog, coyote, or eagle.

16

O. J. Murie
U. S. Fish and Wildlife Service ▶

The sandy plains are the favored home of the kit fox. He ranges in the western portions of North America from southern Baja California, and south-central Chihuahua north through the San Joaquin Valley, northern Nevada, and Great Salt Lake, and through Colorado and western Kansas to parts of southern Canada.

Though his range is rather extensive the kit fox isn't found in large numbers anywhere. Because he isn't very cunning he is easily captured or shot. He has no suspicion of traps as coyotes have; he eats poisoned bait readily. He is at times trapped for his pelt which, according to changes in fur fashion, varies in value from time to time. His is not one of the most desired furs and it doesn't bring much money. Yet men continue to trap him.

The kit fox isn't a harmful animal and he does away with a great many rodents that *are* harmful. He is both rare and interesting, and he deserves more protection than he now gets.

Man will certainly fail to save the California condor unless he tries to save it, and the trying is eminently worthwhile as anyone with even the most rudimentary appreciation of nature will agree who has actually watched wild condors living in their native mountains.

ALDEN H. MILLER

California Condor

~~~~~~

OUR LARGEST soaring land bird is the rare California condor, a vulture. He is about four feet long, weighs about 20 pounds, and may have a wingspread of nine feet. His head is unfeathered, with bright orange skin merging into gray on the neck, where there are patches of red and purple. The feathers are black except on the underside of the wings, which have a broad expanse of white only noticeable when the condor is in flight. His flight is a soaring, majestic action similar to that of the bald eagle.

The condors are carrion eaters. They discover dead

19

animals through their keen eyesight rather than by their sense of smell, then fly to the ground to eat the carrion. Their talons are not made for carrying food.

They gorge at a feeding until filled to sluggishness, then roost in a tall tree until hungry again. While roosting, the head is pulled down close to the body so that it can scarcely be seen.

Condors reproduce their numbers very slowly. Female condors don't breed until they are five years old, and they lay only one egg during the nesting season. The nest is usually in a crack or cave several hundred feet from the bottom of an inaccessible cliff. If they are fortunate enough to rear a young condor chick, that baby condor is dependent upon his parents to bring him food until he is about a year old. Any breeding pair can raise young only every other year.

Condors are among the most sensitive of birds. Any unusual sound or sight within 500 yards of them may make the parent birds stay away from their nest, not caring for their young or their eggs for a day at a time. Thus many eggs fail to hatch, and young birds are left without food to die. Many egg collectors, in their craze to obtain condor eggs, have intruded into the condor territory. Some birds no doubt have been wounded or killed at such times. Some men who would not willingly injure the birds did, nevertheless, seek them out in order to record observations of young birds or nests, also to photograph them.

20

Road building, blasting, and prospecting for oil and uranium cause great disturbance to the lives of these birds.

At one time the condors, being carrion eaters, fed chiefly upon the carcasses of livestock which roamed the western part of our country. As the herds of livestock increased in size and more rangeland was needed, stockmen drove them into more remote regions of the mountains. There the calves were preyed upon by coyotes, panthers, and grizzlies. The stockmen put out poisoned meat in the hope that the predators would be killed off. The condors ate the poisoned meat and died.

In some areas men gave up raising cattle and raised agricultural crops on the land once used for grazing. The lack of cattle carcasses diminished the condors' food supply. Also, men devised better methods of caring for livestock and so fewer of them died, and that action left fewer carcasses to be eaten by condors. Predators on the cattle gradually became fewer, too, and not as many cattle were killed. Often the carcasses were burned or buried before the condors could eat them.

Many condors were shot, simply because they made good targets. The hunters may not have known that these birds did not prey upon other animals, but ate only dead flesh.

The original range of this bird was along the western coast from Lower California to the Columbia River. Then their population began to decrease. No condors were definitely recorded north of California after 1835, and by 1860 they were rarely seen in northern California. Their numbers continued to shrink, and now it is estimated that there are no more than 60 birds left. These are found in Sespe Wildlife Preserve, a rugged mountain area of 54½ square miles in the Los Padres National Forest in southern California. This refuge for condors was established by the United States Forest Service in 1947 to protect the nesting and roosting habitat of this rare bird.

Wildlife experts tell us that the greatest need of the condors is not to have laws passed prohibiting men from shooting them. Rather, these birds can best be protected by being left unmolested in the refuges where they now are. Also, unpoisoned carcasses of livestock should be left at convenient places for the condors to feed upon.

The extinction of the heath hen has taken away part of the magic of the Vineyard . . . there is a void in the April dawn.

HENRY BEETLE HOUGH

Heath Hen

~~~~~~

THE HEATH HEN, also known as pinnated grouse, was a small eastern prairie chicken. In color he was rusty brown above, and white barred with reddish brown below. He preferred to live on dry, sandy plains, among scrub oaks, pines, and other shrubbery. He fed mainly on acorns, grain, and berries.

At the time our country was settled, the heath hen was commonly found in the New England states. Heath hens were such an abundant source of food that people tired of the constant diet of this fowl, even though it was delicate and tasty.

24

American Museum of Natural History

Great numbers of heath hens were killed, and faster than these birds could build up their population. Fewer and fewer of them could be found in hunting season. By 1869 there were no heath hens anywhere in Massachusetts, and by 1870 they were gone from the mainland of New England, and from Long Island. Sometime after 1880 Martha's Vineyard was the only place where heath hens survived. In 1905 only 100 remained. However, a few years later, with rigid protection, the numbers increased to 2,000.

Then a terrible fire devastated the island of Martha's Vineyard. Heath hens and their nests were almost completely destroyed. In the following years their numbers grew fewer and fewer because of predators, disease and other causes. In 1920 there were only 600. In 1928 only 3! In 1930–31 only *one* could be found. This individual was last seen March 11, 1932.

Whether he kills for his own trophy, or to sell the head for money, the poacher of a rare bighorn is one of the meanest of outlaws.

Victor Cahalane

Bighorn

~~~~~~

THE ROCKY MOUNTAIN sheep, commonly known as the bighorn, is one of our rare animals which needs protection. He can be seen only in mountain and desert country of the West and Southwest — the Cascades, Sierra Nevada and Rockies. Rocky wilderness and desert ranges are the natural habitat of the bighorn, who is an imposing figure as he stands on the summit of some jagged mountain ledge.

A bighorn is probably the most sure-footed of all animals, for his hoofs are split and sharp-edged, and concave at the bottom. They act like suction cups to hold the animal's feet on the rocks. He is able to run up and down steep rocky slopes, and even to leap from one rock to another without mishap.

Although a sheep, the bighorn doesn't have a coat of wool like that of a domestic sheep. His coat is hairy, like that of a deer. Bighorns move about in herds, feeding on grass, herbs, and mountain flowers, cacti, prickly pear, and various other kinds of vegetation commonly found on mountain slopes. They don't require great amounts of water, for they get much moisture from the pulp of the plants they feed upon.

These animals have decreased in number since the settlement of western North America. This decrease is due in part to animals which prey upon them — cougar, wolf, and lynx — but partly to loss of forage, as domestic sheep increased in numbers on portions of the bighorn's range. Also, the bighorns caught diseases from the domestic sheep. But the greatest decline in the bighorn's numbers has been caused by hunters. The massive curled horns of the bighorn are considered a rare trophy, and are prized beyond all other trophies. "To kill so rare and beautiful a creature for this purpose," says Devereux Butcher, "is unjustifiable."

Legal hunting of these rare sheep is now forbidden except in certain areas, but the temptation to get a bighorn's head is so strong to some hunters that they risk the penalty

A. Schlechten
U. S. Fish and Wildlife Service

of illegal shooting in order to bring home a prized trophy.

Three sanctuaries have been established especially for the rare desert bighorn, in southern Nevada and southwestern Arizona. Hunting is prohibited there, but poaching still goes on because not enough money is available to hire enough men to do a good patrolling job.

There are other possible dangers to the mountain sheep. Our Air Force has taken over some fairly large sections in the largest refuge and is carrying on gunnery practice there. Also, the Yucca Flats Atomic Proving Grounds borders the largest refuge. Local hunters have demanded that the area be opened to public shooting, and ranchers want permission to set up livestock ranches there.

Persons keenly concerned about the possible fate of the bighorns believe that these animals should be given even more protection than they now have.

The slaughter of animals for pleasure prevents the growth of imaginative sympathy, and blunts all the finer sensibilities of the human mind.

ALEXANDER F. SKUTCH

American Egret

"AIGRETTE" is the French word for plume, and the pure white plumes of the American and snowy egret are his most beautiful and distinguishing identification. These plumes appear on the backs of the male and female egrets only during their nesting season. They look like spun glass and extend a foot or more beyond the tail. At one time these plumes were in great demand for women's hat ornaments and for fans. It was profitable for plume hunters to seek out these egrets during the nesting season when they congregate in large numbers. Hunters killed them even while eggs and young were in the nest, in order to tear the plumes from the birds' backs for women who wanted aigrettes on their hats.

Except during the nesting season egrets are usually

found living in small groups, even migrating in small family groups. They nest in low marshy areas and at the edges of ponds, swamps, and bayous. Their nest is a loose structure of small sticks and twigs, and some nests are located over 100 feet from the ground in the tops of cypress trees.

American egrets are graceful and dignified in movement. They find their food in the water as they stand motionless until fish, reptiles, rats, or mice come near. Then their bills strike out quickly and accurately to seize their prey.

The range of the American egret is temperate and tropical America, and the birds spend winters in the region of the Gulf of Mexico or south of it. At one time in our country the American egrets were present in great numbers. There may have been more than 100,000 egrets in Florida alone before the slaughter of the plumage trade. By 1902 they were rarely seen and were even believed to have been extirpated. The National Audubon Society, founded in 1901, was chiefly responsible for the campaign to save the few remaining egrets its men were able to find. The taking of egret feathers and the marketing of them were forbidden by law. Guards were stationed at nesting colonies to protect the birds from illegal acts of hunters and feather collectors. Gradually the numbers of the American and snowy egret were built up. Without the persistent efforts of the Audubon Society these beautiful birds might never have been seen again in our country.

Like winds and sunsets, wild things were taken for granted until progress began to do away with them.
ALDO LEOPOLD

Woodcock

~~~~~~

THE WOODCOCK is a small bird with a rather long, curved bill. His body is short and chunky. His russet feathers blend in perfectly with his grassy surroundings. Numerous nicknames have been given to this rather shy, inconspicuous bird: timberdoodle, owl snipe, hill partridge, little whistler, and pewee, among others. The woodcock likes privacy. He stays hidden during the day and does his food gathering at night. His curved bill, pushed deep down into damp ground, brings up grubs and earthworms.

The woodcock thrives best in an open growth of mixed

Burley
U. S. Fish and Wildlife Service

hardwood trees near small fields and with a body of water not far away. The birds use the open space among the trees for their courting grounds. The courting ceremony is part of their breeding habits. The male woodcock makes unusual flights which have been called aerial dances. These are performed mainly after sunset and before sunrise, but occasionally go on all night. The male flies upward to 50 or 60 feet in a spiraling motion. Circling, he descends to his take-off spot, uttering a series of twittering calls, seemingly to show happiness and love for his mate. As he alights he droops his wings, spreads out his tail feathers and struts about like a little turkey gobbler, before he takes off in another flight.

The male woodcock needs space for all this activity. If trees are cut down, or if open spaces among trees fill up with brush, the courting grounds become crowded or may disappear entirely. Then the woodcock is forced to seek other places more favorable to his way of life. If the birds cannot find enough places to court and nest and rear young in, they cease to reproduce.

At one time woodcocks were highly prized for their delicious meat. Hunters enjoyed the sport of shooting them, for they made a difficult target. They were so well protected by their coloration among the grass and leaves that anyone could practically step on a bird before he would stir. When he did rise, the sudden take-off into the air was almost straight up. He zoomed off in a whistling flight, twisting in the air as he flew. Keen eyes and an excellent aim were needed to bring down the bird.

As the hunting of woodcocks went on, these birds began to decrease in numbers until in the early 1920's people feared they were nearing extinction. Hunting of woodcocks was prohibited for a good many years. Gradually their population has increased. Even now, states differ in the amount of woodcock hunting permitted, and at what seasons of the year it may be done.

The United States Fish and Wildlife Service is developing some newly forested regions where it is hoped that, by creating suitable spaces among the trees, the woodcocks will be induced to come and do their courting and family rearing. In this way, as well as by protection, the survival of the woodcocks will be assured.

Many of us have an esthetic reason for cherishing the coyote. His song at twilight is almost as typical of the west as were the bison herds and the prairie dog towns. Whenever his quivering wail comes in through my bedroom window it still sends happy little tingles squirming up my spine. It is still the call of the wild to me.

PERCY L. DE PUY

Coyote

~~~~~~

THE COYOTE, often referred to as a "little wolf" and a "brush wolf," is really a wild dog. He lives on the open plains where he finds snakes, lizards, rabbits, mice, squirrels, grasshoppers, vegetables, and even fallen fruits on which to feed. He eats carrion of all kinds.

Coyotes adapt themselves readily to changes of climate and so have been found in both arctic and subtropical regions. They make themselves at home wherever they can find food and sheltering places for their families. Their den is a hole in the ground or among rocks. They are able to

E. R. Kalmbach
U. S. Fish and Wildlife Service

hold their own against both their natural predators and man because they are highly intelligent, fleet of foot, and produce large families. They are clever, alert, resourceful, and tough.

Vast differences of opinion exist among men regarding the value of coyotes. Those who have sheep ranches claim that coyotes are enemies of sheep. Yet the coyote is not first and foremost a sheep killer. Many cattlemen who manage enormous ranges say publicly that coyotes are a benefit to them, for they eat rodents that would otherwise destroy the grass on which the cattle depend for forage. Where cattlemen in Colorado once killed, or allowed others to kill, hundreds of coyotes on their ranges, they now post signs saying, COYOTES PROTECTED. Men at Victorville, California, who raise alfalfa have made it known that they do not want the coyotes in their territory trapped or killed. These men value the services of the coyotes in preying upon rabbits and rodents and in getting rid of carrion. In several counties of Kansas, where poison was widely used to kill off coyotes, it was found that rabbits had increased so rapidly they were becoming a dangerous menace to wheat crops. The farmers in those counties decided that getting rid of coyotes only added to their rabbit problems, and the men stated that coyotes should be allowed to live so that they could "perform the control nature intended."

Many persons believe that the coyote should not be ruthlessly shot, trapped, or poisoned. They concede that the coyote should be controlled in certain localities, but only when there is absolute proof that his killing of animals is harmful in that locality. Many of these persons, no doubt, would agree with Percy De Puy, who says: "I am glad that the little wild dog still haunts the hills and ravines of my native state. May his keen wits and tough adaptability enable him to persist for a long time to come in spite of hunting from automobiles and airplanes, and in spite of the new super poisons!"

If species such as the flamingo are to survive, in the full grandeur of their natural status as wild, free-flying birds, then we must persuade our fellow men that it is time we arranged to share a portion of the earth with them. The results of such an arrangement would be colorful and rewarding beyond all imagination.

ROBERT PORTER ALLEN

Flamingo

~~~~~~

CONSIDERED by some naturalists to be the most spectacularly beautiful bird in the Western Hemisphere, the West Indian flamingo may be facing extinction. Although it has never nested in our country in a wild state, it once occurred in South Florida in large numbers during the off season. Their original home included mainly these places: the Bahamas, Cuba, the Guianas, the Netherlands Antilles, Yucatan, Haiti, and the Dominican Republic.

The beauty of these birds is in their gorgeous color — varying shades of pink and vermilion. The flight feathers

on the edge of the wings are black. The birds weigh from four to eight pounds. The males are larger than the females. A large male may measure six feet from the tip of his bill to his toes.

These birds are distinguished for their very long necks and long thin legs. They have webbed feet. Their bills are large and heavy and crooked downward as if broken in the middle.

Flamingoes feed on tiny molluscs, plant seeds, and mud containing minute animal life. They stir up the mud on the bottom of a shallow pond or inlet in order to loosen the small snails from the mud bottom.

A flamingo sticks his head down into the water where his bill opens so that the top points downward and the tip points upward and backward. He sucks the mud into his bill by means of a pumping action of his throat. At the same time excess water is forced out on each side. The tiny toothlike processes along the bill and on the large tongue strain out the snails and other minute animal life from the mud and water.

The flamingoes are gregarious, and hundreds of them fly together in long, curved lines with necks and legs extended. As they fly they utter loud, honking calls.

These colorful birds use mud for their nests. They scoop up the mud into small hummocks from a few inches to more than a foot in height. They make a hollow in each hummock for the single egg laid by the female flamingo. Parent birds take turns incubating the egg, folding up their long legs as they settle down on the hummock.

At Hialeah Race Track near Miami, Florida, a large flock of flamingoes can be seen, and many of them that were not pinioned have escaped and a few can be seen living in the wild, in Everglades National Park in the southern part of the state. Because they are always seen in a flock they may be thought of as plentiful, but their numbers have dropped dangerously low throughout their range. They are erratic — they change nesting sites unexpectedly; some years they don't nest at all. Their way of life is disturbed by natives who take their eggs and young for food, by hunters, by low-flying airplanes, and by curious visitors to nesting sites, especially photographers. These beautiful birds need our protection.

Every animal, by instinct, lives according to his na-
ture. Every animal is honest. Every animal is straight-
forward. Every animal is true — and is, therefore,
according to his nature, both beautiful and good.

KENNETH GRAHAME

Ivory-Billed Woodpecker

〜〜〜〜〜〜〜〜〜〜〜〜〜〜〜〜〜〜〜〜〜

THE LARGEST woodpecker known in North America
is the ivorybill. It is doubtful that ivorybills are to
be found anywhere in our country now, for it is generally
believed they are extinct.

The ivorybill was a handsome bird, larger than a crow,
with blue-black feathers decorated with dazzling white
patches and a brilliant red crest at the back of the head.
The ivorybill used his three-inch glossy bill like a dagger
as he hammered into trunks of trees and dead limbs for his
favorite food: wood-boring insects and insect larvae. These
are found between the inner bark and the sapwood. Even

46

A. A. Allen
National Audubon Society ▶

though the bark was unbroken and still very tight, an ivorybill could whang away at it with such powerful side blows of his bill that large slabs of bark and splinters of wood were knocked off.

This woodpecker liked solitude, and he chose the deep swampy forests of southeastern United States for his habitat. Cypress, gum, oak, and pine were his favorite trees.

The ivorybills began to disappear about the same time that the trees of the southern swamps were logged off. As the trees went, so went the ivorybills' food supply. Gradually the ivorybills themselves disappeared from the cutover regions. By 1915 these attractive, energetic birds were to be found only in a few localities in South Carolina, Louisiana and Florida. Although there have been scattered reports of ivorybills it is likely that the birds were pileated woodpeckers, which closely resemble the ivorybill. There have been no authentic reports of the ivorybill's existence since 1952.

No humane being, past the thoughtless age of boy-hood, will wantonly murder any creature which holds its life by the same tenure that he does.

HENRY DAVID THOREAU

Manatee

~~~~~~

THE MANATEE, sometimes called a "sea cow," is a slow-moving animal that lives in shallow salt water off the Florida coast. He resembles a seal in shape and may be 15 feet in length and weigh from 600 to 2,000 pounds. His dark gray body, covered with a thick, almost hairless skin, tapers into a tail like that of a beaver. He has only one pair of limbs — the front flippers. His eyes are set in wrinkles and he has no visible ears.

The manatee is a vegetarian. He swims about, feeding under water at times, but he must come to the surface to breathe. Seaweeds and river plants are his chief foods. The manatee pushes these into his mouth with his flippers. His upper lip is divided into two parts and is covered with short, stiff bristles. The manatee makes a great deal of noise while eating. The flapping of his lips and the crunching action of his teeth can be heard 200 yards away.

The manatee isn't a fish, but a mammal. His young are born in late spring and are able to swim immediately. The mother manatee sits up in the water, holds her baby to her breast by means of her flippers, and nurses it. Manatees are very affectionate with their young. Although they usually move away quickly from any danger, they never desert a baby, but gather it up in their flippers as they go. They may thrash their bodies around in the water, causing a lot of hubbub, even flailing about with their tails as a means of defense, but they are seldom aggressive.

Manatees inhabit the warm waters of the Gulf of Mexico and of the West Indies and Central America. We know them best in Florida. Their movements northward are limited by cold weather.

For centuries the flesh of the manatee has been considered a great delicacy. Indians killed manatees with spears thrown from dugout canoes. Eventually white men began to hunt manatees, often just for sport. It was a feat of skill to hit a manatee's head as the animal bobbed about in the water. It has been reported that people out for pleasure

Chicago Natural History Museum

rides in motorboats often fatally wounded the manatees with the boats' propellers. The sluggish animals are often unable to keep clear of boat propellers but in a count of 195 manatees in the Miami River in 1954–55 Dr. J. C. Moore found 57 of these animals so scarred by propellers that they were recognizable as individuals — but apparently none the worse for their experience.

Manatees are protected by law. Much has been learned about these curious animals in recent years, and although they will never be abundant, and are not readily observed, their chances of survival are considered very good.

My most earnest wish has been to stop the extermination of harmless wild animals; not for their sakes, but for ours, firmly believing that each of our native wild creatures is in itself a precious heritage that we have no right to destroy.

ERNEST THOMPSON SETON

Walrus

~~~~~~

THE WORD "walrus" comes from "valross," meaning whale horse — a name given by Norwegian sailors to this large, rather ugly marine animal. Walruses are massive creatures with small heads and bristled muzzles. Their hide is thick and wrinkled and covered with dark brown hair. Their length varies from 10 to 12 feet, and their weight is well over 2,000 pounds. The weight of a male from Walrus Island, Alaska, was 3,432 pounds.

The walrus is distinguished from his relatives, the seals, by long ivory tusks, which are yellowish white in color and protrude downward from his jaws. These tusks may be any-where from 14 to 30 inches long and weigh from six to nine pounds. They serve two purposes: self-defense and digging sea food from the floor of the ocean. A walrus uses his two pairs of flippers to propel himself about in the water. Although he is an accomplished swimmer, he must at times rest on land or ice.

The habitat of the walrus is the Arctic Ocean near Spits-bergen south to Newfoundland, and the Bering Sea near the Pribilof Islands. Moving in herds, they drift down from the Arctic Ocean into the Bering Sea in autumn and back to the Arctic in May or June. During that time each female walrus gives birth to a single baby called a "pup."

The walrus's most feared predator is the killer whale, yet men destroy more walruses than killer whales do. Eskimos long have hunted walruses for their meat, blubber, oil, and hides. They carve the animal's tusks into beautiful orna-ments.

Long ago the Eskimos did their necessary hunting of walruses with harpoon and lance. They killed what they needed, and there was little mass slaughter of these ani-mals. Now, with the use of high-powered rifles, many more walruses are being killed, and much faster.

At one time walruses were plentiful on Sable Island near Nova Scotia and as far south as Massachusetts Bay. Walrus

William Sholes
U. S. Fish and Wildlife Service ▶

hunters killed so many of these animals that around 1650 none were left on Sable Island.

Now the United States, Canadian, and Russian governments must regulate the kill of walruses and limit the exportation of their tusks. It is estimated that there were some 200,000 Pacific walruses alone up to about 1790. The present population is some 45,000.

The present range of the Pacific walrus is in waters adjacent to Alaska and Chukotski Peninsula, from Barrow on the east to the East Siberian Sea on the west.

The Atlantic walrus now occurs sparsely from the Canadian Archipelago east to Greenland, Spitsbergen and the Laptev Sea. It is now seldom found south of Hudson Bay.

*We doubt if the existence of whooping cranes makes
the slightest difference to the balance of nature or to
the destiny of man. But it's comforting to think that
there are still people who can take profound interest
in such things as the nesting habits of the whooping
crane. It helps maintain and fortify whatever sanity
remains.*

Editor of *Toronto Globe and Mail*

Whooping Crane

THE WHOOPING CRANE is usually spoken of in terms
like these: "rarest bird in all the world"; "beautiful
and spectacular"; "America's most magnificent bird." Yet
he is threatened with extinction. Mr. John K. Terres says:

No one knows when the whooping crane became a white,
shining, five-foot-tall bird. Perhaps it has always been the
superb creature that it is today. Combined with its tall stature,
its white feathers glistening like snow in the sun, the glowing
red skin patches on its head, and its almost fierce, yellow eyes,
the whooping crane has something else. It has *character*.
Through the ages it has gained a wild wisdom, a keen and
knowing awareness that has made it the wildest, wariest creature on earth. High in courage, ready either to battle or to lead

away any animal foe in defense of its mate or young, yet, it is almost helpless before its most dreaded enemy — modern man. Unable to cope with the rifle and shotgun, unable to adjust to the creeping tide of humanity that crowds closer and closer, the last whooping cranes have retreated into a vast Canadian wilderness. There, in an ancient way known to all wild things, and to man himself, they perpetuate their kind by raising families of young cranes that will replace the older ones when they have died. But the struggle of these last few whooping cranes — perhaps less than 20 — is more than a fight for a few cranes to live. It is a battle against extinction from which these beautiful creatures, once they are struck down, never rise again.

For a half century the existence of the whooping cranes has been a precarious one. They first started to lose their nesting habitats when men ploughed up the grasslands to make farms, and drained the prairie sloughs. Now they winter on the Arkansas National Wildlife Refuge in Texas, arriving there in late October and early November. At the refuge they are protected from hunters, and they feed upon crabs, shrimp, snakes, and small fish.

In April whooping cranes fly north to their breeding grounds in a corner of Wood Buffalo Park in Northwest Territories, Canada, in the region of Great Slave Lake. There a mated pair "stake out" a territory about a mile in diameter which they claim as their own. They announce their ownership with loud buglelike blasts which give them their name, "whooping crane." They build a large nest, a

58

W. F. Kubichek
U. S. Fish and Wildlife Service ▶

platform of grass and reeds, and the female lays two big buff-colored eggs which take 33 to 34 days to hatch.

In late September the whooping cranes begin their return journey to the refuge in Texas. They always follow a particular route, about 2,500 miles long, passing through Saskatchewan, the Dakotas, Nebraska, Kansas, Oklahoma, and Texas. It is on their migratory journeys that they are most likely to lose some of their numbers. In the past many were shot by hunters, but today protection and the cooperation of sportsmen is close to 100 per cent perfect.

Wildlife authorities who are eager to save this bird suggest several ways in which help may be given. More information about identifying whooping cranes and reasons for protecting them is being widely circulated by state and provincial game departments and by Audubon Societies to encourage hunters not to shoot them. All places visited by whooping cranes on their migratory journeys, especially on the Platte River in Nebraska and certain areas in Kansas and Saskatchewan, should be established as permanent refuges for these and other migratory birds.

Results of efforts to give this beautiful, rare bird protection have been encouraging. A report from the U. S. Fish and Wildlife Service in December, 1958 indicates there were 32 whooping cranes on the wintering grounds at the Aransas Wildlife Refuge — 23 adults and 9 young. Counting the six in captivity, the Service says the total in existence is 38. This is the highest number of whooping cranes since the first count of them in 1938.

Public opinion is working today for the whooping crane. Why could it not be aroused for the Everglade kite? If we fail to do something now, only ghostlike wraiths of the bird will drift by on the breezes that sweep the Florida marshes — silent, fading, dying — no more than visionary phantoms in the memories of men who have known this gentle, harmless creature.
ALEXANDER SPRUNT, JR.

Everglade Kite

〰〰〰〰〰〰〰〰〰〰〰〰〰〰〰〰〰〰〰〰〰

MORE GRACEFUL and more beautiful than a hawk, and completely harmless, the Everglade kite has constantly been shot *as* a hawk, even though in flight he doesn't resemble one. Now this bird, whose range in the United States has been shortened to certain parts of Florida, is threatened with extinction. Reported as abundant in 1895 in most of the fresh-water marshes of Florida, the Everglade kite's numbers have declined until it is estimated that there are less than a dozen in Florida and the whole United States today. However, in some areas of Cuba,

Mexico, Central and South America these birds can still be seen in considerable numbers.

The Everglade kite is a handsome, dark-feathered bird, with square tail, white rump patch, bright red legs and eyes, and a slender, hooked bill. He is an unusual bird in that he feeds on only one type of snail, the Pomacea, which is found in fresh-water marshes. Because of the habit of eating only this snail, the Everglade kite has been called a "snail hawk." The kite flies low over the saw grass of the marshes in a steady flight, head tipped down, looking for these snails. When a snail is sighted, the bird swoops down to seize it in strong talons, then flies to a convenient perch, extracts the snail, tears it apart, swallows it, and drops the shell onto the ground below.

This unusual feeding habit may result in the disappearance of this kite from Florida and the United States. By draining the marshes to put land into use for agriculture and for development purposes, people have deprived the Everglade kite of his sole source of food. Even when a marsh is reclaimed, it may be a long time before the Pomacea snails reappear.

Thoughtless egg collectors who invade the marshes and take the Everglade kite's eggs are also responsible for killing off this harmless bird. While some young kites continue to be hatched, the number of these birds is declining.

Those who have studied the problem believe that the

Everglade kite may someday disappear from the Florida scene. If this is to be prevented it will be necessary to establish sanctuaries where suitable habitat of sufficient size can be fully protected and controlled, and water levels maintained even in time of drought by pumping from underground springs. In addition, the dwindling kite population might be increased by the introduction of these birds from their range farther south.

Too often the mean, blinding, loveless doctrine is taught that animals have neither mind nor soul, have no rights that we are bound to respect, and were made only for man, to be slaughtered or enslaved.

JOHN MUIR

Wolf

~~~~~~

THE WOLF is a wild dog resembling the German shepherd dog. He has a heavy frame with large long forelegs and feet. His head is broad and blunt. An adult varies in weight from 30 to 100 pounds or more, and in total length from four to seven feet. The dog teams used in Arctic regions are usually made up of dogs that have some wolf blood. This wolf strain gives the dogs a ruggedness and endurance much needed for the work they do.

Wolves usually travel in packs of from 50 to 100 animals as they search for food. They are predatory and feed largely upon small mammals, such as mice, ground squirrels, rabbits, and pocket gophers. Occasionally they run down and kill larger prey, but mostly the animals they seize are the weaker ones. A herd of elk in a protected wilderness became stronger and more numerous when wolves killed the weaker members. Wolves will eat carrion when no fresh meat is obtainable. Naturalists testify that wolves seldom attack people unless they are attacked first.

The wolf is a kind and loyal mate, and the male wolf has been called a tender, conscientious father. The mother wolf takes good care of her cubs and can be savage when man or animal tries to harm her young. Female wolves often adopt orphan cubs to rear as their own offspring. Numerous stories have been written telling of the devotion among wolf family members.

Lois Chrisler in her book *Arctic Wild* tells how she came to know wolves through personal experience. Wolves became her companions and revealed characters that were marvelous and gentle.

Wolves have long been considered savage killers, and have been feared and hated. Because wolves sometimes kill livestock, men have often tried to exterminate them, and through widespread killing these animals have disappeared from nearly all settled parts of our country. They cannot be found now except in some of the northernmost parts of a few midwestern states and parts of Canada and Alaska.

In spite of the strong feeling against wolves, they are a part of our wilderness and, as such, deserve protection from extermination.

U. S. Fish and Wildlife Service

The true conservationist is compassionate to all living things, refraining from wantonly injuring them and helping them to live by preserving conditions favorable to them.

JOSEPH WOOD KRUTCH

Sandhill Crane

~~~~~~

THE SANDHILL cranes are attractive birds with slate-gray bodies and naked, red foreheads. They stand about 3½ feet high. They once lived in most parts of this country, but they were hunted so persistently for their delicious flesh that now they are found in only a few places east of the Mississippi, except in Florida, where they may be increasing. They nest on the grassy flats or tundra of northern Canada and Alaska, and they winter as far south as California, Texas, Mexico, and Central America.

Sandhill cranes divide their time between land and water. Sometimes they are seen around the still waters of open marshland, wading on long, slender legs, feeding on fish, frogs, and salamanders. On dry land they eat lizards, mice, snakes, grasshoppers, and occasionally grain in the fields. As they stride about in a deliberate, dignified way

Howard Zahniser
U. S. Fish and Wildlife Service ▶

they seem the calmest of birds, but they are among the wariest, always alert to the faintest sound or sight that may suggest danger. When alarmed, they run a few steps, then take off into the air with strong, rhythmic flaps of their wings, and a characteristic flick on the upbeat. Their wing-spread may be six and a half feet. They can be identified in flight, for they always fly with neck and legs stretched out in line with the body. They have been called "flying crosses."

As a sandhill crane flies, he utters a loud, wild, guttural cry that can be heard long after he has disappeared from sight. This haunting note comes from an amazing wind-pipe, part of which is coiled and twisted within the breast-bone region. From the lungs to the throat this windpipe averages about 27 inches.

Of all the birds who perform courtship dances during the mating season, probably none is more amusing to watch than the sandhill crane. At that time the sandhill cranes seem to lose all their calm and dignity. An eyewitness of their courting dance told how the birds bowed and dipped and leaped high into the air, drooped their wings and cir-cled about, hopping, skipping, and calling loudly. Actually sandhill cranes often dance silently, without any use of the voice. When they do call, it is usually a single "garoos-a-a-a" call, according to Walkinshaw.

When the nesting season begins, each pair defends a certain territory of its own in a swampy place. The female sandhill crane lays two or three eggs in a nest, which is a depression in the ground lined with grass and weed stems. The male and female take turns sitting on the olive-colored eggs for a 30-day incubation period. The young birds hatch out covered with a coat of down, and in a few hours they can run about. Then they are taken by the parents to a drier piece of land. Now the whole family feeds on roots and stems, insects, berries, frogs, and crayfish. The young birds start making short flights about two months after hatching. By the third month they join the adults behind their trumpeting leader and all set off on the southward flight in single file or V formation, often shifting into straight or wavy lines as they travel. They keep calling as they fly, welcoming other sandhill cranes who join them. They stop now and then to rest and feed. In the Great Plains and Pacific Coast states there are many favored places where they stop. In the past they were widely hunted.

Like many other large birds, cranes must be given special protection. Drainage of marsh areas for agriculture and long seasons of drought have destroyed many of their feeding and nesting places. Illegal hunting has taken its toll. But wildlife refuges, stricter laws regulating hunting, and general education about these birds have helped to keep them alive. More people must become informed about the habits and needs of the sandhill cranes if they are to survive as a species.

*That the Great Auk no longer exists, and that you
and I will never see one living in its former habitat
has no effect on our daily lives; but just as the world
would be poorer were the music of Chopin obliter-
ated and no one again could hear it, so the world is
poorer because no one ever again will see the huge
auk colonies that once thrived on little Funk Island.*
DEVEREUX BUTCHER

Great Auk

~~~~~~~~~~~~~~~~~~~~~~~~~~~~~~~~~~~~

LITTLE FUNK ISLAND off the east coast of Newfoundland was once the home of huge colonies of great
auks. Standing about two feet high, and dressed in black
and white feathers, they resembled penguins. A great auk's
legs were placed so far back on his body that the bird
seemed to stand on his tail. His wings were so small he
could not fly, but he was an excellent swimmer and diver.
He swam under water, using his short legs as paddles, pur-
suing and catching fish for his food. He could move fast
enough to elude sharks and other predators in the water.

From our earliest history, great auks were known on the

rocky coasts of northern North America. They were first discovered around 1497 by French fishermen who came to the Newfoundland coasts. The great auk colonies were a plentiful source of fresh meat and eggs so that it was considered unnecessary to stock much food on the fishing boats.

Cartier reported that on his first voyage to Newfoundland in 1534 he had visited an "island of birds" (probably Funk Island) and that his men filled two boats with dead birds in less than half an hour. In addition, every ship salted down five or six barrelfuls.

The down of the eider duck had always been a great source of supply for feather beds and coverlets, but about 1760 there was a great shortage of eider ducks, and feather hunters turned to the great auk colonies. Records tell us that several crews of men once lived all summer on Funk Island, killing these birds in huge quantities.

During spring and summer the great auks nested on the rocky islets off the coasts of Newfoundland and Iceland and the Gulf of St. Lawrence. In winter they migrated by swimming under water as far south as Florida. In the spring they returned to the rocky islets, which were reached by walking in from the ocean. Each female great auk laid one spotted egg, about five inches long, on bare rock. After the eggs hatched, the young ones followed their parents to the ocean, where they spent the rest of the spring and summer, swimming, diving, and feeding on fish.

These birds were clumsy and slow-moving on land, so that while they were congregated on the rocks they were an easy prey. Their sense of hearing was very keen. They were easily alarmed by any strange noise, but not by the sight of a person. If the birds had eggs or young on the rocks they stayed by them. As a consequence, the great auks were clubbed to death by the thousands. Finally, about 1844, the last one was killed.

Robert S. Lemmon writes in his book *Our Amazing Birds:*

The world has seen many instances of man's reckless destruction of other forms of life which surrounded him, but somehow the case of the Great Auk is particularly discreditable. That millions of such harmless, half-helpless birds should have been exterminated primarily to provide food for white men's stomachs and feather beds for them to sleep on is a far from pretty picture for us to acknowledge.

To kill a beautiful creature that has the same right to live as we, is wrong. To force a creature to give up his life merely to prove oneself a marksman, is indefensible.

DEVEREUX BUTCHER

Key Deer

〜〜〜〜〜〜〜〜〜〜〜〜〜〜〜〜〜〜〜〜〜〜

THE FLORIDA KEY DEER is one of the harmless forms of wildlife which needs protection if the species is not to be exterminated. Key deer belong to a geographic group, the white-tail deer, but are the smallest member of that group, and one of the smallest deer in the world. They are only about 39 inches long from tip of nose to tip of tail, and they stand 26 to 29 inches tall. Adult bucks average about 50 pounds in weight.

Key deer live on the little subtropical islands (keys) between Key West and the mainland of Florida amid such tropical surroundings as wild orchids, palms and cacti, crocodiles and alligators. They swim from key to key in search of food and fresh water. Of all the keys, Big Pine probably offers the best living conditions for them. It has

76

John D. Dickson III
Florida Game and Fresh Water Fish Commission

an abundance of different kinds of wildlife food plants as well as pockets of limestone rock formation which hold fresh water the year round.

At one time in our country's history these attractive little animals were numerous in the Florida Keys. Christopher Columbus reported seeing a stag, the first deer his party saw in America. But hunters have been killing key deer without regard to season of year so that these animals have been almost wiped out. Men did not like to follow the key deer through the junglelike habitat. Often they set the tall grass afire to drive the deer into the water, where they could be shot more easily. Sometimes the men sent dogs into the swamps to run the deer to exhaustion. When the frightened animals leaped into the water for safety, the hunters, stationed in boats, shot them.

Many friends of wildlife became alarmed over the possible extermination of this harmless and beautiful species of deer. By 1949 their estimated number was as low as 30. They faced extinction. Interested persons worked to have a refuge established for them. Many attempts were made, many discouragements resulted. But in 1957 Congress passed an act to preserve the key deer. This act authorized the establishment of a National Key Deer Refuge not to exceed 1,000 acres. This area will be protected from fire, and from illegal hunting and trespassing. With these safeguards the key deer are increasing in number. The present population is thought to be around 100 animals.

Can Society, whether through sheer wantonness or callous neglect, permit the extinction of something beautiful or grand in nature without risking extinction of something beautiful and grand in its own character?

Christian Science Monitor Editorial

Trumpeter Swan

～～～～～～～～～～～～～～～～～～～～～～～～～～～

THE TRUMPETER SWAN is the largest waterfowl in the world and also one of the rarest. These birds are found only in North America, and have been so greatly reduced in number that they are seldom seen. They are distinguished by jet-black bills that contrast sharply with their pure white plumage, and by a resounding trumpeting call. The swan can make this sound because he has an extremely long windpipe, part of which is coiled within the bird's breastbone.

The life cycle of trumpeter swans is an interesting one. They do not migrate long distances, but stay rather close to the breeding grounds, seldom journeying farther than 100 miles. Early in the spring breeding pairs take up residence in frozen marshes before the ice goes out. As soon as the water is free of ice, nest building and egg laying begin. A cob (male) and a pen (female) as a mated pair claim a certain large nesting territory and are keenly alert to defend their claim. Five eggs is the usual number laid in each nest. The incubation period lasts about 35 days. When baby swans are hatched they are covered with mouse-gray down and they do not acquire the full white plumage until they are three years old. They pair at that time and breed a few years later. They are rather long-lived. Some have been known to live for over 30 years.

In the 1700's the trumpeters were a familiar sight to the early settlers and trappers of our country. These swans were an impressive sight, too, flying in great V-shaped wedges or placidly swimming on some isolated mountain lake. They were fine targets because of their size, color, and habit of flying rather low. Hunters shot them for their flesh and their feathers. Records of the Hudson's Bay Company in the years between 1853 and 1877 show that over 17,000 swan skins had been sold, a great number those of trumpeter swans. By 1900 this bird was considered to be extinct.

About 1919 a few isolated breeding pairs were seen in and around Yellowstone Park. This discovery led to a campaign in the early 1930's to save the trumpeter from threat-

Ray C. Erickson
U. S. Fish and Wildlife Service

ened extinction. Part of the campaign was the establishment, by the U. S. Fish and Wildlife Service, of the Red Rock Lakes Migratory Waterfowl Refuge in southwestern Montana. This refuge is a wilderness marsh of about 15,000 acres, and it has been important in the fight to save the swans. From a small flock of 100 these rare birds increased to 763 in 1958. This figure included 147 cygnets, young-of-the-year.

At Lincoln, Nebraska, the only known trumpeter swans in captivity can be seen at the waterfowl pond in Pioneers Park. Two birds were found crippled by shot and were nursed back to health. They were presented to the park and are now on daily exhibition. The wings of the birds have been clipped so that they cannot fly away.

The trumpeter swan is by nature a wilderness bird. It prefers a natural, shallow marsh habitat far from people and their activities. The number of these beautiful swans is now growing slowly but steadily, mainly because some of the citizens of our country acted in time to conserve one of the most impressive waterfowl species in the world.

What is a little loss of sport to us compared with the extinction of a species — something that the hand of man can never replace?

WITMER STONE

Eskimo Curlew

〜〜〜〜〜〜〜〜〜〜〜〜〜〜〜〜〜〜〜〜〜〜〜〜〜〜〜

CURLEWS ARE large shore birds with down-curving bills. The Eskimo curlew was the smallest of these, between 12 and 14 inches long. His bill was only slightly curved and varied from 1½ to 2½ inches in length. All curlews have brownish coloration, streaked with cinnamon brown, but the darkest colors of the Eskimo curlew were on his back and the top of his head. The tips of the feathers were buffy brown and the linings of the wings also, making this bird conspicuous when he was in flight. The call notes of the Eskimo curlew had a squeaking sound which identified him among other curlews. In New England he was given the name "bee bird."

The migrations of these curlews were extensive. In the fall they assembled by the millions along shores of Labrador and Newfoundland. They fed greedily on berries and snails, getting fat in preparation for their trip south. Then they set off on what was a tremendously long journey, to Nova Scotia, then south to Argentina and Patagonia. It is believed that for most curlews this was a nonstop flight. Their return journey in the spring took them to the Gulf States and up the Mississippi Valley to Canada. A single flock, alighting in Nebraska, was reported to have covered from 40 to 50 acres of ground.

From records kept about Eskimo curlews we learn much about their mass migrations and the killing of them in mass shootings. The Boston Society of Natural History stated in its record for 1906–7:

> On the 10th of August, 1860 the curlews appeared along the North Atlantic shore in great numbers. We saw one flock which may have been a mile long and nearly as broad; there must have been in that flock four or five thousand. The sum total of their notes sounded at times like the wind whistling through the ropes of a thousand ton vessel.
>
> But we met with none during our visit to the Labrador coast in the summer of 1906. We talked with many residents and they all agreed that the curlew, though formerly very abun-

84

dant, suddenly fell off in numbers, so that now only 2 or 3 or none at all might be seen in a season. Captain Parsons of the mailboat *Virginia A. Lake* said that curlews were very abundant up to 30 years ago. He often shot a hundred before breakfast, often killing 20 at a single discharge. Fishermen killed them by the thousands. They kept loaded guns at their fish stages and shot into the flying masses, often bringing down 20 or 25 at a discharge.

Curlews made delicious eating and were avidly hunted wherever they appeared. Experienced gunners could kill a whole flock of these birds at one time, and wagonloads of dead curlews were commonly seen during spring and fall migrations. The number of these birds rapidly declined.

By the late 1890's people in North and South America were certain that the Eskimo curlew was headed for extermination. Efforts to give this species protection didn't come in time to save them. A few individual birds have been reported in various places since then, but there is no hope that the Eskimo curlew will survive. He must be counted among those harmless species of wildlife which man has destroyed.

*No living thing was created without reason. No wild
animal walks with aimless feet.*

GENE CAESAR

Wolverine

~~~~~~

THE LARGEST member of the weasel family, this
"super-weasel," as the wolverine is often called, is
renowned for his ferocity, strength, and cunning. Hunters
and trappers in the early days of our country's history considered the wolverine their greatest obstacle in accumulat-
ing pelts. The wolverine removed bait from traps, and
even freed the trapped animal. He sometimes hid traps or
destroyed them. He was too clever to be enticed into a
trap, himself.

This animal, for his size, is the strongest mammal in
North America. Weighing from 18 to 40 pounds, his pow-

erful body is set upon short, squatty legs. His hair is long and dark and coarse; his face is brown with a gray forehead; his tail is long and bushy; his claws are long and white and exceedingly sharp.

A wolverine is a solitary animal, ill-tempered and self-sufficient. He never hibernates or stores up food for stormy days. In winter his fur coat grows thicker and his feet become cushioned with stiff hair soles. He can endure a very cold climate, and his search for food keeps him on the move the year round. His appetite is prodigious. He will kill young animals which he digs out of their burrows; he may rob nests of their eggs and young. He invades trappers' cabins to eat all the food supplies there. He eats carrion wherever it is found. He also likes wasp larvae, snails, insects, and rodents.

Wolverine fur is not considered valuable in this country, but the Arctic region natives prefer it to all others. It makes an especially fine trim for hoods and cuffs of parkas because the guard hairs of the wolverine do not accumulate frost. The natives once considered the fur a mark of distinction and believed that the wearer of the pelt would be endowed with some of the strength and cunning of the wolverine.

Men have hunted wolverines ever since the beginning of our country's history, and they have almost extirpated the species. No wolverine has been seen in Michigan, the

New York Zoological Society Photo

Wolverine State, for a hundred years. It has been 40 years since wolverines were known to be in the New England states. There are a few in Glacier National Park, the Sequoias, and the Sierra Nevadas. Yet at one time these animals were numerous and their range extended north from Maryland to the timber line, and westward to the Great Lakes and on to the Pacific.

Many people believe that the wolverine should be protected. Through his superior strength, exceptional courage, and unusual cunning, he has won a place for himself in the animal world.

Once you have seen the spoonbills flashing their pink and carmine wings against the blue of a Florida sky you'll get some idea of the satisfaction of those who have fought to protect this bird.

ROBERT PORTER ALLEN

Roseate Spoonbill

~~~~~~

RADIANTLY beautiful pink and carmine feathers and an odd, spoon-shaped bill distinguish the adult roseate spoonbill from other birds. The bird's neck is long and white; the short tail is a striking orange buff; the long, thick legs are red. The head has no feathers on it.

The roseate spoonbill is one of the most beautiful birds in North America. He originally nested in many locations along the Gulf Coast, especially in Florida. The spoonbill lives in a variety of coastal habitats — dry islands as well as wet marshy sites on the Texas coast, bulrush marshes in

Louisiana, and mangrove islands in Florida Bay. Their bulky nest may be built on the ground or eight feet high in a red mangrove.

The roseate spoonbills were never killed for their feathers, which fade rapidly when plucked. They were the innocent victims of plume hunters who raided mixed colonies and shot out the egrets. The spoonbills were driven from their eggs and young by the disturbance. By 1890 they had disappeared from Texas. By 1902 only a few were left in Florida. They were thought doomed in the United States.

Fortunately for the roseate spoonbill and for us, the Audubon Society took vigorous action to protect whatever birds remained. Laws were made to protect the roseate spoonbill permanently. Wildlife sanctuaries were established in Florida where those birds could find refuge and good nesting sites. By 1935–36 there were 30 nesting adult roseate spoonbills in the Florida Bay area, the only breeding area of this bird in that state. By 1954–55 this critically small number had increased to 428, but loss of feeding areas as a result of real estate development in the Florida Keys reduced this number to 300 in 1958 and 1959.

Roseate spoonbills gradually returned to Texas, undoubtedly flying there from the coasts of Cuba, Mexico, and South America. They travel in flocks, in long, diagonal

Allan D. Cruickshank
National Audubon Society ▶

lines. But many casualties occurred among these birds on the Texas coast during 1942–45. Local training fields there were engaging in aircraft target practice. The spoonbills, congregating in open, unprotected areas, were often intentional or accidental targets, and the flocks diminished. Recovery has been encouraging, however, and the Texas-Louisiana flocks by 1959 totaled more than 2,000 birds.

The roseate spoonbills, like all wading birds, must get their food from the water. They will be in danger if water areas are drained or filled. They feed on small fish, shrimp, and water insects from shallow water along the coasts and in ponds of fresh water. The spoonbills submerge their heads while feeding, swinging their spoonlike bills back and forth through the water as they wade on their long red legs. Anything edible caught in the bills is soon swallowed. The young roseate spoonbill takes predigested food from the throat pouch of the adult, reaching into the side of the mouth to avoid the wide, spoon-shaped bill.

Their future existence is in jeopardy for many reasons. Some of their natural feeding areas are being dredged and filled, turned into boat basins and building lots. If the birds are to continue to find food, a new natural feeding area must be reserved for them.

More and more, people are becoming concerned about the difficulties facing the roseate spoonbills. Some towns consider these lovely birds one of the star attractions offered to tourists. Robert Porter Allen, who lives in the town of Tavernier, Florida, says in his book *On the Trail of Vanishing Birds:*

Today this community is proud of the fact that this is the only town in the United States where roseate spoonbills are a daily sight in winter. You can see them feeding in ditches along the highway, and you can stand in front of the drugstore and point them out to visitors. "Look, right overhead, there goes a spoonbill."

*The destruction of the wild pigeon and the Carolina
paroquet has meant a loss as severe as if the Catskills
or the Palisades were taken away. When I hear of
the destruction of a species I feel as if all the works
of some great writer had perished.*

THEODORE ROOSEVELT

Carolina Paroquet

〰〰〰〰〰〰〰〰〰〰〰〰〰〰〰〰〰〰〰〰〰〰〰〰〰

THERE ARE probably no Carolina paroquets alive
today. We can best learn of their beauty through
paintings of them showing their brilliant green, yellow,
and orange plumage. They were a species of parrot, and
the only species known to have lived in our country. They
ranged over the Atlantic Coast States from Florida to New
York, west to Texas, Oklahoma, and eastern Colorado, and
north as far as Iowa and Wisconsin.

The Carolina paroquets were partial to heavily timbered
swamplands and particularly to trees with hollows in them.
These hollows provided fine nesting and roosting sites.

96

Some of the hollows had been excavated by large woodpeckers. If the holes were too small to admit the body of the paroquet, he roosted by hanging to its edge with his strong claws and bill.

The Carolina paroquets were about the size of the mourning dove. They were swift and graceful in flight, flying in large flocks, uttering shrill, metallic sounds very unpleasant to the human ear.

They fed in the early morning and early evening, taking berries, fruit, seed balls of sycamore and cypress trees, wild grapes, pecans and beechnuts, and even young grain and citrus. As early as 1714 a man from the Carolinas wrote about the paroquets: "They visit us first when mulberries are ripe, which fruit they love exceedingly. They peck the apples. They are mischievous to orchards."

Farmers and fruit growers may have felt justified in killing many of the Carolina paroquets because the birds sometimes destroyed complete orchards, and even young grain and citrus. At feeding time they seemed almost tame and could easily be approached by netters and hunters. The brightly colored feathers made good targets among the tree branches. The birds provided good eating, and besides were sold to the millinery trade. Also, because of their beauty people wanted to keep these birds in cages, so paroquets were trapped and netted for that purpose.

Unluckily for the paroquets, they had either a large

curiosity or compassion for a companion in distress. If one paroquet was shot, and fell to the ground, the others of a flock, instead of flying away, hovered about him. Thus they were easily killed. Due to widespread killing and trapping, these friendly, beautiful birds gradually declined in numbers. The last ones seen were in Florida. There has been no proved record of their existence since 1904.

We have already outgrown such cruel sports as bear baiting and dog fighting, and it seems likely that some day we will renounce hunting as a form of amusement.

RICHARD H. POUGH

Musk Ox

~~~~~~

BUILT LIKE an ox and with a slightly musky odor, the musk ox is well named. He lives the year round in the bitterly cold Arctic regions. His outer coat is of long dark shaggy hair sometimes a foot in length and matted close for warmth. Under this is a second coat of dense fur which neither cold nor moisture can penetrate. The protruding eyes are almost hidden by long hair. He has a hump similar to that of a bison. His legs are very short and he weighs around 500 pounds. His horns are a formidable weapon. They are thick and curved and meet at the top of the head where they flatten out and form a sort of shield.

100

Frank Dufresne
U. S. Fish and Wildlife Service

Musk oxen travel about in small groups, foraging as they go, on the meager vegetation of the Arctic: grasses, mosses, lichens, and some small shrubs. As winter approaches they move to places that give them some protection from icy winds. They eat frozen plants, using their hoofs to scrape away the snow that covers them.

The female musk ox usually breeds only every other year, and then gives birth to a single calf. Because of the severely cold climate into which baby musk oxen are born, many die at birth. A band of musk oxen often has only three or four cows of breeding age, the other animals being males or young ones. This means that only three or four new offspring are produced in any one year.

At one time these shaggy animals probably existed in huge numbers in the Arctic regions. Eskimos depended upon them for their flesh, milk, hides, and bones. The milk is said to be as good as cow's milk, and the flesh has a fine flavor. Men in the crew of Admiral Peary's expedition to the North Pole in 1899 shot many musk oxen. Mr. Peary said, "I never associated the idea of sport with musk oxen — too often in the years gone by, the sighting of those black forms has meant the difference between life and death. The finding of a herd saved the lives of my entire party."

This species is losing out in its struggle for existence. It is estimated that the total number of musk oxen is now only about 20,000 animals. As men have gone farther afield in their explorations and have shot musk oxen for sport, these animals have slowly begun to decrease in numbers. The high-powered rifle in the hands of Eskimos and white men alike has made it possible to kill these animals more easily. When the musk oxen sight or scent danger they form a compact circle of bodies with heads pointing outward, and never retreat from the danger. A hunter with his high-powered rifle can shoot a good many at one time. Unless the animals are hit by bullets in the brain or spine, they will stand for a long time while bullets are pumped into their bodies before they finally drop.

In the past, much needless killing has gone on because of the capture of musk ox calves. In the early 1900's the zoos of our country and Europe wanted musk ox calves. The calves are so closely protected by the older animals that hunters had to kill many adult animals before they could obtain one calf.

Many persons are now alarmed about the possible extermination of the musk ox. Shooting these animals for any reason whatsoever is prohibited. Canadian Royal Mounted Police investigate every report of musk oxen having been killed. The United States Fish and Wildlife Service has helped to re-establish musk oxen in southwestern Alaska and it reports that a herd of them in the Nunivak Island National Wildlife Refuge has increased in 20 years from 31 animals to 126. This isn't a very rapid or a very large increase, but with constant vigilant protection the musk ox may be helped to make a comeback.

All birds and beasts and creeping things fly from man's approach. They know his civilization means their destruction.

JOHN C. VAN DYKE

Labrador Duck

~~~~~~

WE ARE TOLD that the Labrador duck is extinct, but no one seems to know why. The last known one in existence was killed on Long Island, New York, in 1875.

Specimens of the Labrador duck are on display in museums, and from these specimens we know that this waterfowl was a handsome bird, particularly the male, who wore striking black and white plumage, with an almost solidly white head. The female duck was less showy, with grayish-brown feathers on the upper part of the body and grayish-white underneath.

104

American Museum of National History

The Labrador ducks are believed to have bred on the rocky coasts of Labrador and the Gulf of St. Lawrence. Some were found on the sandy shoals off the New England coast. They fed mainly on shellfish. The Labrador duck's feathers, like those of the eider duck and the Great Auk, were much sought after for stuffing pillows and feather beds. It may well be that overhunting of these birds caused the extermination of the species. "It is significant," wrote Edward Howe Forbush, "that the Labrador duck's extinction occurred in the nineteenth century when marked improvements in firearms were accompanied by the extermination of far more species of birds than in any other century since the dawn of history."

*There will always be pigeons in books and in muse-
ums. . . . Book pigeons cannot dive out of a cloud to
make the deer run for cover, or clap their wings in
thunderous applause of mast-laden woods. Book
pigeons cannot breakfast on new mown wheat in
Minnesota, and dine on blueberries in Canada. They
know no urge of seasons; they feel no kiss of sun, no
lash of wind and weather.*

ALDO LEOPOLD

Passenger Pigeon

No ONE has seen a passenger pigeon since 1914, for
at that time the last one died in a Cincinnati zoo.
The passenger pigeon was a graceful, beautiful bird, resembling our mourning dove, only much larger. The male
bird was handsomely feathered in slate blue and brown on
his back; his head was blue, his legs red. On the side and
back of the neck pink, purple, green, and gold feathers
glistened in the sunlight. A long, wedge-shaped tail gave
him slenderness.

Around 1800 these pigeons were the most numerous of
all birds in our country. They lived together in enormous

flocks. In Michigan a nesting area extended 28 miles in length and over three miles in width. In another region nesting sites covered about 100,000 acres. The nests were placed in high trees, sometimes as many as 50 to 100 nests in a single tree. The nesting trees were often used as roosting places. The trees provided food, too, and it is said that no caterpillars or inchworms could be found in the nesting oaks for several *years* after the pigeons had nested there.

When leaving the nests to feed or flying to their roosting trees, the pigeons soared aloft in such numbers that they could blot out the sun. People watched in amazement as flocks swung through the skies as far as eyes could see in every direction. Equipped with marvelous vision, these birds could identify desirable food from a great height. They roamed far and wide over our country searching for food, which was abundant then — berries, soft fruits, insects, and worms in summer; acorns and beechnuts in the fall and winter.

The wing muscles of passenger pigeons were large and powerful, considering their body size, and they could average a speed of a mile or more per minute. The birds migrated south in the fall, north in the spring, not so much because of changes in weather as because of changes in the available food supply. The largest flocks usually passed over a given place in three days. Other flocks continued to come for several weeks longer.

American Museum of Natural History

John James Audubon described a flight of passenger pigeons he saw in Kentucky. The birds passed overhead for three hours without any interruption in a mass extending about a mile in breadth. He estimated the number of birds to be about 1,115,136,000.

Often a flock stopped its flight to roost in trees for the night. The birds alighted one above another on branches in such masses that sometimes the branches broke from the weight.

It was easy to kill these birds because they congregated in huge flocks. They were so plentiful and their flesh was so delicious they were shot by hunters in great quantities. Men decoyed the pigeons into traps and nets and then shot or clubbed them to death. They suffocated some with sulphur fumes. In northern birch forests where pigeons roosted, the trees were set afire. When the birds leaped from the trees for safety they were caught and fed to hogs. Even when there was no need for the pigeons to be shot as food, they were killed anyway, for they made an easy target.

As the railroads advanced westward the netters followed the birds more easily. More than a million pigeons were shipped to market in a single year. As many more were dried, smoked, or pickled for winter eating.

By 1878 the last great migration of passenger pigeons was ended. By 1890 only a few stray flocks of these lovely birds remained in this country. People began to realize that this needless killing would end in the birds' extermination. Many men worked to get a law passed forbidding hunters to shoot passenger pigeons. But plans to save this bird came too late to do any good. In 1908 the only known survivors were placed for safety in a Cincinnati zoo. A price of $1,000 was offered for a male and female pair, in the hope that new stock could be produced so that the species would not die out. But no passenger pigeons could be found anywhere on this continent, and on September 2, 1914, the remaining one in the zoo died. All the laws that men can make, and all the sanctuaries they can set up now, will not bring this species back to life.

A man is ethical only when life, as such, is sacred to him, that of plants and animals as well as that of his fellow men, and when he devotes himself helpfully to all life that is in need of help.

ALBERT SCHWEITZER

Grizzly

〰〰〰〰〰〰〰〰〰〰〰〰〰〰〰〰〰〰〰〰〰〰〰〰〰

CALIFORNIA's state animal — the grizzly bear — seen on that state's flag, has not been reported in the state since 1922. All over the western part of the United States the grizzly has been so relentlessly destroyed that the species may become extinct. This "King of the Wilderness" is considered by some men to be the most unpredictable and the most dangerous of all game animals. Perhaps that is the reason why it is the most sought after and the most highly prized by hunters.

Before the exploration and settlement of the West, many thousands of grizzlies roamed the mountains and plains.

112

Now it is believed that only about 750 grizzlies survive within our Western states, especially Washington, Colorado, Wyoming, Idaho, and Montana. It is estimated that 10,000 survive in Alaska, and many thousands more in Canada.

The grizzly wears a loose-fitting fur coat. He averages from 400 to 600 pounds in weight, but has been known to weigh as much as 1,000 pounds. His shoulders are humped and the hair on his back and sides is tipped with silver, giving him a frosty appearance. His tail is very short. His legs are short, too, but very powerful, and he walks flat on the soles of his feet, which have long, heavy claws, slightly curved. Though his body is heavy and his legs are short, the grizzly can run rapidly for a short distance. He can outrun a horse in the first one hundred yards. While he is said to have a savage disposition, he attacks a man only when he has been cornered or provoked.

The grizzly is omnivorous, feeding on both vegetable matter and animal flesh. He likes grass and roots, fruits, berries, insects, honey, and fish. He digs out small rodents from their burrows. He preys upon sheep and cattle. He will eat carrion.

Grizzlies don't reproduce in great numbers. Females do not mate until they are three or four years old. They mate only every other year and they normally give birth to only two cubs. Much killing has been done not only by game hunters but also by sheep ranchers and cattlemen who shot the grizzly as a menace to their livestock. Thus the species is dangerously close to being extirpated in our Western states.

In two states action is being taken to help the grizzlies survive. Colorado has gone all-out to protect grizzlies. The State Fish and Game Department officials there declared the grizzly to be a nonhuntable animal, and a grizzly refuge was established. A onetime Fish and Game Commissioner of Wyoming has said, "There are an estimated fifty grizzly bears left in this state. Present laws and regulations permit 85,000 persons to hunt these animals — 1700 hunters for each grizzly. In the past four years our grizzly population has been reduced fifty per cent. We must decide whether we wish to exterminate them or whether we wish to manage them in select areas in controlled numbers as a native game animal worth preserving. Another year or two of indecision, and there will be no decision left to make."

The government of Alberta once thought it was necessary to protect people from grizzlies; now it feels that grizzlies are the ones to be protected — from people. The government has set aside an area of 8,000 square miles of land in northern Alberta which is to be a game reserve for these mighty "Kings of the Wilderness."

There is at stake in this particular instance not only the fate of a great bird, but also the human capacity to tolerate, to appreciate, and to enjoy.

Olaus J. Murie

Bald Eagle

~~~~~~

AT REST or in flight the bald eagle is a never-to-be-forgotten sight. In repose he is an impressive figure. He sits on a lofty perch, erect and proud, the white feathers on head and neck gleaming in the sunlight, his piercing yellow eyes concentrating on some object far below him which may become his prey.

In flight he soars effortlessly in the highest reaches of the sky, his wings stretched out to a span of six feet or more, turning and curving in a series of graceful spirals. Edwin Way Teale, the great naturalist, describes the bald eagle in flight as "writing the poetry of motion on a blue page of sky."

The eagle chooses his mate for life. Their nest is usually

Bob Revels
Florida Game and
Fresh Water Fish Commission ▶

in a tall tree on the shore of lake, stream, or along the coast line. Each spring, before the eggs are laid, a mattress of dried vegetation is piled on top of the framework of sticks to cushion the eggs. Two or three eggs are laid in the nest and the parent birds take turns incubating them. When the eggs hatch, the parents spend about four months caring for their fledglings. They never go far from the nest except in search of food.

The favorite food of these eagles is fish, which is the reason the nesting tree is usually near water. In Alaska, where fish are abundant, a check was made of the bald eagle's feeding on salmon. The records show that while these birds do catch some live salmon as they swim up-stream to spawn, they also eat many salmon that die before they reach the end of their journey as well as those who die soon after spawning. Other animals the bald eagle catches as food are rabbits, squirrels, woodchucks, weasels, and snakes. The prey they catch is torn by their beaks and talons into pieces that the young eagles can swallow easily.

Young bald eagles do not have the white feathered heads, necks, and tails of the adults. They are all brown. It takes them four to five years to mature, when the feathers of the head, neck, and tail become white.

The birds return to the same nest year after year. Since bald eagles live to be very old, and since each year a new nest is piled on top of the former one, it may become very large. Near St. Petersburg, Florida, a nest has been in the process of building for some forty years. It is now 20 feet high, its flat top measures about nine and a half feet across, and the nest must weigh several tons.

In June, 1772, when the Continental Congress of the United States sat in session in Philadelphia, one question before them was "What bird shall be our emblem?" Whatever bird was chosen, they agreed, should be worthy of the nation it would symbolize. It should represent strength, power, loyalty, majesty, and freedom. After due deliberation the assembled men made their decision: The bald eagle should be our national emblem. No other bird in the United States embodied all those characteristics.

At the time the bald eagle was selected as our national emblem, he could be found over all the United States except in the more arid regions, but over the years he has been extirpated from most of his range. In the 175 years following his selection as our national symbol, the bald eagle has been persecuted everywhere in this country. He was shot for sport and with the mistaken idea that an eagle as a bird of prey should be killed whenever possible. When the hunters could not get close enough to a bald eagle to shoot it, they robbed its nest of eggs or young. It even became profitable for men to shoot our national bird. In some places bounties were paid for each pair of talons brought in. In the years between 1917 and 1952, about 115,000 bald eagles were killed.

Today the bald eagle is found mainly in Alaska and Florida. Hundreds of thousands of citizens have never seen, and may never see, the great bird which represents this nation.

About 158 years after the bald eagle had been honored by the Continental Congress, he was given the protection he deserved in 48 states. It took 12 years more before this protection was extended to Alaska — the place where so many of his kind had been slaughtered. That protection finally came in 1952. Our Federal Government has enacted laws that provide for a fine up to $500 for harming our national bird. At long last this noble bird is under the protection of strict laws. Still, he may never increase to his former numbers.

The future of bald eagles in Florida is partially dependent upon what happens to the land there. In the extensive development programs going on in that state, as forests of cypress and pine are replaced by houses and farms, the eagles will naturally become less numerous.

Many naturalists are convinced that the bald eagle will make his last stand for existence within a few years, and that stand will be on public lands set aside as national parks and wildlife refuges. If his last stand is successful, thousands of us who have never seen this proud bird except on the Great Seal of the United States may see him alive, soaring high in the sky, over the great nation which he represents.

A Hopeful Outlook

~~~~~~

If you have been saddened as you have read the stories of these species of wildlife in danger, you will be heartened by the knowledge that there is a hopeful outlook concerning them.

There is in our land a new, encouraging attitude toward wildlife. More people than ever before have a kindlier awareness of wildlife's part in nature's plan for all living things. "We, the people," says Dr. Olaus Murie, "are beginning to feel the wholesome impulse of generosity toward our fellow creatures."

In addition to *feeling* differently, people want *to do*

something. Many acts of thoughtfulness and generosity are being performed that will help assure life and safety to wildlife. More laws are being passed to restrict hunting, trapping, fishing, and netting. Many public and private agencies are at work turning back to swampland certain areas which never should have been drained, thus inviting some kinds of wildlife to take up residence there. Land that once grew trees but which was overcut or burned is being replanted to forests. Wherever soil, water, trees, and grass are being wisely used, wildlife thrives.

More states are enacting laws to protect eagles, hawks, and owls. Refuges are being established where adequate care is assured for wildlife. More young persons are taking to the outdoors to "shoot" wildlife with a camera instead of with a gun.

There is a steady increase of interest in and appreciation for wildlife shown by young people all over our country. This is apparent in the activities of such organizations as Boy Scouts, Girl Scouts, Campfire Girls, and Junior Audubon Society Members, to name only a few.

Every person, young or old, can enjoy the wildlife about him and do something to help preserve it. Perhaps in time everyone, young and old, may become imbued with the belief held by Alan Devoe that "we are brothers of all living things." Alan Devoe writes:

We could survive and continue to eat three meals a day if all the whooping cranes were extirpated. We are not going to die of hunger or thirst because there are no ivory-billed woodpeckers. But the conserving of such creatures as these is an inseparable part of life as a whole. This life of ours all goes together. Trees and water and land and birds, mammals and fish and snakes and everything else, from our own dooryard to the farthest reach of the farthest wilderness.

Whooping cranes are not in themselves an immediate factor in our security as a biological organism. But ultimately and to some degree their fate touches upon ours. In a much more than poetic sense we are brothers of whooping cranes. We are brothers of all mammals, all birds, all living things.

A Statement of Audubon Philosophy

We believe in the wisdom of nature's design.

We know that soil, water, plants, and wild creatures depend upon each other and are vital to human life.

We recognize that each living thing links to many others in the chain of nature.

We believe that persistent research into the intricate patterns of outdoor life will help to assure wise use of earth's abundance.

We condemn no wild creature, and we work to assure that no living species shall be lost.

We believe that every generation should be able to experience spiritual and physical refreshment in places where primitive nature is undisturbed.

So we will be vigilant to protect wilderness areas, refuges, and parks, and to encourage good use of nature's storehouse of resources.

We dedicate ourselves to the pleasant task of opening the eyes of young and old that all may come to enjoy the beauty of the outdoor world, and to share in conserving its wonders forever.

REFERENCES

Allen, Durward, *Our Wildlife Legacy*. New York: Funk & Wagnalls, 1954.

Allen, Robert Porter, *On the Trail of Vanishing Birds*. New York: McGraw-Hill, 1957.

Audubon, John James, "The Passenger Pigeon" from *John Kieran's Treasury of Great Nature Writing*. Garden City: Hanover House, 1957.

Audubon, John James, *Birds of America*. New York: Macmillan, 1941.

Bodsworth, Fred, *The Last of the Curlews*. New York: Dodd, Mead, 1955.

Butcher, Devereux, *Seeing America's Wildlife in Our National Parks*. New York: Devin-Adair, 1955.

Cahalane, Victor H., *Mammals of North America*. New York: Macmillan, 1947.

Crisler, Lois, *Arctic Wild*. New York: Harper & Brothers, 1958.

Greenway, James C., Jr., *Extinct and Vanishing Birds of the World*. New York: American Commission for Wildlife Protection, New York Zoological Park, New York, 1958.

Hegner, Robert, *Parade of the Animal Kingdom*. New York: Macmillan, 1935.

Johnson, James Ralph, *The Last Passenger*. New York: Macmillan, 1956.

Kieran, John (ed.), *John Kieran's Treasury of Great Nature Writing*. Garden City: Hanover House, 1957.

Krutch, Joseph Wood (ed.), *Great American Nature Writing*. New York: Wm. Sloane Associates, 1950.

Lemmon, Robert S., *Our Amazing Birds*. Garden City: American Garden Guild and Doubleday and Co., 1952.

Leopold, Aldo, *A Sand County Almanac*. New York: Oxford University Press, 1949.

Menaboni, Athos and Sara, *Menaboni's Birds*. New York: Rinehart and Co., 1950.

Pearson, T. Gilbert (ed.), *Birds of America*. Garden City: Garden City Publishing Co., 1936.

Peterson, Roger Tory, *Birds Over America*. New York: Dodd, Mead, 1948.

Rand, Austin J., *American Water and Game Birds*. New York: E. P. Dutton, 1956.

Sprunt, Alexander, Jr., D. Sc. *Florida Bird Life*. New York: Coward-McCann and National Audubon Society with co-operation of U.S. Fish and Wildlife Service and Florida Game and Fresh Water Fish Commission, Copyright, 1954 by National Audubon Society.

Wilson, Alexander, "The Carolina Paroquet" from *John Kieran's Treasury of Great Nature Writing*. Garden City: Hanover House, 1957.

Magazines

Audubon Magazine

Broley, Charles L., "Plight of the American Bald Eagle." July-August 1958.

Devoe, Allen, "Why Bother?" Nov.-Dec. 1948.

Errington, Paul L., "A Closer Look at the Killers." July-August 1958.

Hyde, Dayton O., "My Greater Sandhill Cranes." Nov.-Dec. 1957.

Jackson, Hartley, "The Return of the Vanishing Musk Oxen." Nov.-Dec. 1956, Jan.-Feb. 1957.

Morrison, Kenneth D., 'Bird Protection Laws Show Progress." Sept.-Oct. 1955.

Murie, Olaus J., "Wolf." Sept.-Oct. 1957

——————, "Last of the Big Bears." July-August 1958.

Terres, John K., Men, Hope, and Whooping Cranes" (editorial). Sept.-Oct. 1955.

Wagner, Robert, "Life with the Captive Whooping Cranes." Sept.-Oct. 1956.

White, Col. Robert Bruce, "The Wolverine." Mar.-Apr. 1958.

Nature Magazine

Barrette, Keith, "A Trumpeter's Winter Resort." January 1956.

De Puy, Percy L., "The Coyote and his Menu." March 1957.

Latham, Roger M., and Liscinsky, Stephen A., "Life with the Timberdoodle." November 1956.

Rutter, Russell J., "Voice of the Wolf." May 1958

Skutch, Alexander F., "Nature's Harshness and Man's Compassion." March 1956.

Westwood, Richard W., "What is the Whooper's Future?" (editorial). January 1957.

————————————, Hunting is Being Oversold (editorial).

The Grade Teacher

"The Bald Eagle." February 1959.

Miscellaneous

Christopherson, Edmund, "The Case of Our Vanishing Grizzlies." *Saturday Evening Post*, Sept. 20, 1958.

Cooney, R. F., *The Grizzly Bear, Our Endangered Wildlife*. National Wildlife Federation, Washington, D.C.

Fading Trails, New York, Macmillan, 1942.

Kartwright, *Ducks, Geese, and Swans of North America*. Washington, D.C., 1943.

National Wildlife Federation, *Our Endangered Wildlife*. National Wildlife Federation, 1956.

Schaffer, Dick, "Plight of the Whooper," *Outdoor Nebraska*, Fall, 1957.

Smelser, Marguerite A., *Predators — Kill 'Em or Keep 'Em?* Sponsored by San Bernado Valley Audubon Society, San Bernardino, Calif., 1956.

Special Scientific Report #4, *The Pacific Walrus*, USFWS, 1958.

Sprunt, Alexander, Jr., *Vanishing Wings Over the Sawgrass. Audubon Magazine* reprint, Nov.-Dec. 1950.

U. S. Fish and Wildlife Service, *Key Deer Progress Report*, May 1958.

Walkinshaw, *The Sandhill Cranes*, 1949.

ACKNOWLEDGMENTS

I acknowledge my indebtedness and gratitude:

To the many outstanding writers whose works listed in the references have inspired me, and to those whose lines I have quoted.

To the photographers whose superb photographs illustrate this book.

To Robert Porter Allen who read the manuscript and offered valuable criticism.

To the Editor of Audubon Magazine *for permission to quote from the article: "Why Bother?" by Alan Devoe, November-December, 1948; and from the editorial: "Men, Hope, and Whooping Cranes" by John K. Terres, September-October, 1955.*

To The Grade Teacher *for permission to reprint the article "The Bald Eagle," February, 1959.*

INDEX